Praise for *Coconut Milk*

"McMullin's style is sometimes conversa~~~~ ~~~~ ~~~~ ~~~es fo-
cused on the poetry on the page. He has ~~~~ ~~~~ ~~~~ ~ages, and I appre-
ciate his refusal of translation. He balance~ ~~~ ~age, and the erotic through his
words."

—Qwo-Li Driskill, author of *Sovereign Erotics: A Collection of Two-Spirit Literature*

"We islanders from within the Polynesian Triangle that runs from Aotearoa to Hawaiʻi
to Rapa Nui can be found, seen, and heard within the words and between the lines of
Dan's inspiring poetry. His significant work ought to be spread throughout the USA
and be as visible as tiki bars! A real tiki cannot be found within a bar, but you can expe-
rience an authentic one right here in Dan's beautiful art/heart. A must read!"

—Rena Owen, Maori actress, writer, and director

"McMullin's *Coconut Milk* is a brilliant collection of both narrative and avant-garde
poems descended from traditional storytelling that give voice to Samoan Faʻa Fafine
culture as it continues to flourish in Samoa and in the colonial diaspora."

—Brandy Nālani McDougall, author of *The Salt-Wind: Ka Makani PaʻAkai*

"With searing perception, honesty, and lyricism, Dan's words dance off the page and
find their way to our hearts. Poignant, moving, dynamic in scope, *Coconut Milk* is but
a window into the harsh realities that face Samoans and Pacific Islanders who have
navigated the geography and psychology of living in and for America. From boyhood
innocence on an American territory, to coming of age discoveries, to the complexities
of a closeted existence, to his own adult liberation, Dan's story is ours. It is our histo-
ry. Our herstory. Our struggle. But most importantly, the political, the violence, the
vulnerabilities, the cultural awakenings, the juxtapositions, the paradoxes, the contra-
dictions of *Coconut Milk* are our song of survival. Essential and crucial, *Coconut Milk*
should be tasted at tiki bars, universities, backseats of cars, church halls, community
centers, raw food restaurants, gay bars, straight bars, any bar, war zones, military bases
,and especially in the halls of Congress, where it should be required reading! And to
Pacific Islanders both at home and in the diaspora, *Coconut Milk* just cleared the path.
MegaLOVE!"

—Sia Figiel, author of *Where We Once Belonged*

"Dan Taulapapa McMullin's poems come at you with a beguiling openness, honesty,
irony, humour, and compassion. I love their surface simplicity, which draws you into
their profound complexities of meaning and feeling. In short, I love them."

—Albert Wendt, author of *Leaves of the Banyan Tree*

"It was a sharp wit that grated the pithy coconut meat of American Samoan Fa'a Fafine intelligentsia experience and observation to produce the fine material in this collection of poetry. There is incisive cultural and political theorizing taking place here that holds its own with the best of scholarly insights. But there is also a sumptuous sexiness that oozes through the poems. The indigenous peoples of the Pacific Islands region have long known the nourishing qualities of coconut milk. With Dan Taulapapa McMullin's new collection of poetry, I predict readers will find themselves in the position of both being luxuriously sated and panting for more."

—Teresia Teaiwa, author of *Searching for Nei Nim'anoa*

"Acerbic, vibrant, jocose and profound all at once—like any Fa'a Fafine worth her salt— *Coconut Milk* is an illuminative meditation on identity, culture, and history. It is also a powerfully personal collection. Tracing the interstices between Samoan and Western concepts of gender, sex, and spirituality; charting the presence of our ancestors in the contemporary world—like all great poetry, it is impossible to read Dan Taulapapa McMullin without learning something about oneself."

—Daniel Satele, Samoan artist and writer

"Hey Queerdo . . . this book will save your life. McMullin is a masterful comedian + storyteller of immense + terrible beauty. *Coconut Milk* is nondairy genius + bullshit free. Soak it in now + repeat again + again."

—Joël Barraquiel Tan, author of *Type O Negative*

"Tiki decor, as the advert says, can remind you and your customers of an exotic and tropical climate. The question posed by Dan Taulapapa McMullin's *Coconut Milk* is whether we want to be reminded of an exotic and tropical climate, that is to say, of the reality of an exotic and tropical climate, which may be humid, might be fetid, could be bee-stung with breezy beauty, as foreign and falsely friendly as our very own backyards and as our own sense of family, who we keep, at our peril, in our backseats. Where you might, at your peril, keep these bristling lines."

—Vanessa Place, author of *Statement of Facts*

"Just as coconut leaves can be woven into various patterns, McMullin weaves multiple languages and poetic forms to address themes of migration, gender, colonialism, and sexuality. At the book's sacred center lies the rich meat: the 'fa'afafine,' an identity within Samoan culture that McMullin shows is much more complex, intimate, erotic, beautiful, humorous, and natural than simply being 'gay.' Throughout, the unfolding waves of words press and sieve the coconut meat into milk and oil, which nourish the Pacific body and give it a 'fa'afafine shine.' When you open the shell of this book and drink from its mouth, you will be kissing the eel. You will be kissing 'the sea filled with rainbows.'"

—Craig Santos Perez, author of *From Unincorporated Territory [Saina]*

Coconut Milk

Volume 76

Sun Tracks

An American Indian Literary Series

Series Editor

Ofelia Zepeda

Editorial Committee

Larry Evers

Joy Harjo

Geary Hobson

N. Scott Momaday

Irvin Morris

Simon J. Ortiz

Craig Santos Perez

Kate Shanley

Leslie Marmon Silko

Luci Tapahonso

Coconut Milk

Dan Taulapapa McMullin

THE UNIVERSITY OF
ARIZONA PRESS

TUCSON

The University of Arizona Press
© 2013 Dan Taulapapa McMullin
All rights reserved

www.uapress.arizona.edu

Library of Congress Cataloging-in-Publication Data
McMullin, Dan Taulapapa.
[Poems. Selections]
Coconut milk / Dan Taulapapa McMullin.
pages ; cm. — (Sun tracks : an American Indian literary series ; volume 76)
ISBN 978-0-8165-3052-6 (pbk. : acid-free paper)
I. Title.
PS3613.C58546C96 2013
811.6—dc23
                        2013009921

Publication of this book is made possible in part by the proceeds of a permanent endowment created
with the assistance of a Challenge Grant from the National Endowment for the Humanities, a federal
agency.

Manufactured in the United States of America on acid-free, archival-quality paper containing a
minimum of 30% post-consumer waste and processed chlorine free.

18   17   16   15   14   13   6   5   4   3   2   1

Contents

Coconut Milk

J, She, and the Eel

J always stayed in the kitchen
       That's what fags in American Samoa do
       take care of the young and old,
       haunt the kitchen, cooking
       and washing dishes

Now, this part of the story I made up
One day
       a missionary gave J an eel to cook
       but J knew it was a sacred eel
       and was taken by it
He kept it in a rain barrel filled with water
       as a pet

A sacred pet

This other part's real again
Every once in a while
       J put on a bright frock
       beat her face and caught a taxi to town
Pago Pago!

As She she went to all the clubs
       and asked all the straight boys to dance
       because she only danced with straight boys
And of course they all did
       because you know
       it's impolite to a person's entire family
       to say No

Meanwhile
       the sacred eel
       grew larger and larger
       until its head was the size of a coconut
She screamed and
       made a pond to hold it

This part's true
One day
       She decided to form her own club with all the fa'afafine on the island
They called themselves the Daughters of Samoa

She grew her hair long
       dyed it red
       and got a job as Executive Secretary to the President
       of American Samoa Community College
       which she runs to this day

And the ending I made up
One night
       the sacred eel grew so large
       (as tall as a coconut tree)
       that it chased She
       from village
       to village
       through
       all
       of
       Sa
       Moa

Sa Moana Poem Number One

When I was a small boy in San Pedro California
lying around on the bed in the afternoon with my young Mom Lupelele
looking at movie star magazines I thought Liz and Marilyn

were almost as beautiful as my Mom
and my favorite activity in the world was to listen to her dress for work or something special
the smell of lipstick, nylons, and perfume coming around the door

When she was ready
she would ask me to zip up the back of her dress
the journey of my life began there

Sa Moana Poem Number Two

When Dad went to the American War in Vietnam
Mom took us home for our first time to the Samoa Islands on Pan Am Airlines
Me and my brothers in our JFK suits and crewcuts
Mom and my sister in Lady Jackie gloves and dresses

The blue and white airplane doors opened to dawn
As in rushed green heat of rainforest and warm tropic sea
My uncle the doctor drove us in a station wagon with cracked windshield
Thru miles of breadfruit, mango, guava, coconut, hibiscus, cacao

Everyone from my mother's village was out to greet us dancing singing
Every fale home covered in flowers, vines of flowers twining the church pillars
My tamafai sister waited shyly for us among the blooms having arrived earlier
Already changed like we would soon be, brown and free, heart wild as a bird in flight

My grandfather's house was the one half western dwelling, a Dr. Seuss house to me
Open doorways and windows, no doors or glass, flight of steps on the outside of the building
No railing, where were we? Not in Asia, not in Europe, not in America anymore, in a dream
The part of the movie that is in color, black and white before and after, now Oz, Atlantis, Mu

My great-grandmother, a hundred years old, hard as firewood
Leaning into her single piece of cloth wrap, reached down at me, "Kalofae, si kama!"
Was all the spark I needed to send me screaming down our muddy village road
Where another relative came out of the trees, leg swollen barrel size by elephantiasis

Wee queen me running over rotted leaves, past lawns covered that year with frogs
Recently imported by a brilliant palagi to eat all the mosquitoes, now mosquitoes and frogs by legions
Then I stopped before a gaping hole in the earth lined with red hot stones
Above which tall muscular men, black in the shade of the trees, threw in leaves as long as themselves

Coming from the corral my grandfather ordered everyone about, and two hogs were brought down the hill
I looked them in the eye, as both pua'a were killed
With wooden clubs raised overhead by beautiful men, kirikiki clubs come down in thunder
Was the world split in two, our feast, welcome home, to black out, a song

Dear me days in hospital, one fever after another, families waiting on woven mats in the halls
In the children's clinic a box of comic books in American English more familiar than the world outside

And then I returned at last to join my brothers and sisters, my mother, now one with savages
Our pallor once cultivated in European rooms lost, hot chocolate skin in the rain
Sliding down the hillsides into split oil drum boats dropped from the footbridge in the stream
Shooting thru the village to the sea, white sand, blue waters, dumping pig guts for the wild fish

Sa Moana Poem Number Three

When I was young, in California, I drove my mother everywhere
                                because she didn't drive a car there
She always sat in the backseat
                        as we carried on our conversations and destinations
Me driving in the front seat
                like a chauffeur
                        but used to her way that way

Later in life I lived in Samoa again
                                my best friend and I drove all over the islands
While she sat in the backseat
                and I in the front seat driving
Finally, one day, I said
                "You know my mother used to always do that"
"Do what?"
                "Sit in the backseat while I drove her around sitting in the front seat"

"Well you know,"
                my friend said
"In Samoa, this is a sign of respect
                        to the driver"

Sa Moana Poem Number Four

I was with a woman friend
                       visiting my mother

Mom really wanted nothing better than for my woman friend and I
                                      to get married and set me straight
While sitting at my desk in the loft doing something
                            I can't remember what
I overheard my woman friend in the living room say
                       to my mother
      "Dan
         has the mind
             of a woman"

Sa Moana Poem Number Five

Once when Hollywood came to Samoa to make a black-and-white movie
My aunt Tutasi made friends with the filmmakers
She went to Hollywood and became a contract player at Paramount Studios
But spent most of her time showing her All American movie star friends like Dorothy
Lamour
How to look and act like Polynesian dusky maidens
Until Tutasi tired of never getting her close-up because she looked really dusky
Tired of dodging falling coconut trees in wide shots of hurricanes for lighting checks
She asked her boyfriend George Raft for help
George was the only movie star playing gangsters who actually was once a gangster
She took the Red Line to Laguna Beach with George to visit his ex-girlfriend Bette Davis
As soon as they walked in Bette handed her baby to Tutasi to babysit
Putting her arm in George's heading out to dinner without my aunt
Later Tutasi overheard Bette say to George

I can't help her
                        she isn't one of
                                    us

Tiki Manifesto

Tiki mug, tiki mug
My face, my mother's face, my father's face, my sister's face
Tiki mug, tiki mug

White beachcombers in tiki bars drinking zombie cocktails from tiki mugs
The undead, the Tiki people, my mother's face, my father's face
The black brown and ugly to make customers feel white and beautiful

Tiki mugs, tiki ashtrays, tiki trash cans, tiki kitsch cultures
Tiki bars in Los Angeles, a tiki porn theatre, tiki stores
Tiki conventions, a white guy named Pupulele singing in oogabooga fake Hawaiian
       makes me yearn to hear a true Kānaka Maoli like Kaumakaiwa Kanakaʻole
       sing chant move his hands the antidote to tiki bar people
       who don't listen because tiki don't speak any language
       do they

Tiki bars in L.A., in Tokyo, in the lands of Tiki, Honolulu, Papeʻete
Wherever tourists need a background of black skin brown skin ugly faces
       to feel land of the free expensive rich on vacation hard working
       with a background of wallpaper tiki lazy people wallpaper
       made from our skins our faces our ancestors our blood

Yes it's all wrong but looks like my great grandmother's fale sort of
       except she isn't here and it doesn't really, her fale
       didn't have a neon sign blinking for one thing

And yes it looks like Polynesian sculpture sort of not really but what
       is the difference, the difference is this, we didn't make it
       or if we did it was someone desperate but probably not any of us
       just someone making a buck carving shit for drunks

The difference is this, our sculpture is beautiful, tiki kitsch sculpture is ugly
       not because they look so very different but because their shit
       is supposed to be ugly
       because we are supposed to be ugly
       and if we are ugly then they are beautiful
       American or European or Australian or Asian or
       a lot of us too and anyone can be beautiful and expensive
       as long as tiki kitsch is on the walls looking ugly and cheap

I like going to tiki bars sometimes and hearing island music or
       doing island karaoke and there are tiki bars in the islands sort of but

there they're just bars and I'm here in Los Angeles or anywhere here
in the so-called West which is everywhere
and here there, we are tiki mug people, my mother's face, my father's face
my face, my sister's face

Our Tiki sculptures are based on our classic carvings, which are abstractions, idealizations
of beauty, our beauty, though in these bars they are . . .
Well, you get it

Can I remind us that Tiki
Whom we call Ti'eti'e and Ti'iti'i
Some call Ki'i, some call Ti'i

That Tiki was beautiful, jutting eyebrow, thick lips, wide nose
brown skin in some islands
black skin in some islands
brown black deep, thick thighs
jutting eyebrow, thick lips, wide nostrils, breathing

Lifting the sky over Samoa, lifting the sky over Tonga
lifting the sky over Viti, lifting the sky over Rapanui
lifting the sky over Tahiti, lifting the sky over Hawai'i
lifting the sky over Aotearoa, and looking to, paying respects
to Papua, to the Chamorro, to Vanuatu, to Kiribati
lifting the ten heavens above Moana, not your Pacific, but
our Moana

And now in tiki bars Chilean soldiers have drinks from tiki mugs after shooting
down Rapanui protestors in Rapanui, not Easter Island, not Isla de Pascua
but Rapanui, whose entire population was kidnapped and sold in slavery
to Chilean mines in the 19th century, and whose survivors are shot on the streets
of their lands still just a few days ago in 2011 in Rapanui

And American police drink mai tais in Honolulu bars from tiki mugs while
native Hawaiian people live homeless on the beaches

And Indonesian settlers drink from tiki mugs in West Papua where 100,000
Papuans have been killed seeking freedom after being sold down the river by
President Kennedy so he could build some mines for his rich cultivated
humanitarian friends

And French tourists drink from tiki mugs in Nouvelle-Calédonie and Polynésie française
while native people are . . .

Where? Where are we?
In the wallpaper, on the mugs?

'O Kaulaiku

Tasi	**Lua**	**Tolu**
Let's go into the forest		
	I'm afraid	I'm not afraid
There are cacao fruit		
with sweet seeds to suck		
There are breadfruit trees		
which means baking of		
course		
There are plump birds		
who sing so sweetly		
you can almost hear them		
say		
yes dear		

There are tiresome vines	I'm afraid of dying	I'm not afraid of
and battlements	I'm afraid of arguments	anything
There are old land mines	I'm afraid of mailing	Except when someone
with the imperialists'	postcards	is standing in the
compliments	I'm afraid of seeing treetops	distance
There are shattered trees	I'm afraid of. I'm afraid of	I'm very afraid of seeing
and giant stinging bees		someone standing in the
		distance
		I'm afraid of that

And beyond is an old		
temple		
	I know the place	I don't know the place
	It's forbidden	Let's go
It's really just a clearing		
	It's evil	
They used to dance there		
long ago		
	They ate people!	

Tasi	Lua	Tolu
That's not true		Well they stopped
I don't think it's true		Didn't they?
Oh, let's go		Oh, let's go
Tonight		
	No	No
	We should finish husking these coconuts	It might be fun
I'm done	I'm afraid I'm not done	I'm done
Let's wait here under this tree	It's getting dark	
I can hear the ocean	I can hear the ocean	I can hear the flying fish
	What's that there?	
It's my grandparents' tombstone		
They were buried together		
If you stand here at midnight		
you can hear them singing their hymns		
They were a serious couple		
	I don't want to hear them singing	I heard someone singing yesterday
It's dark enough now	So let's go back	
Follow me		Let's go
	It's dark up here	
	Darker than I thought it might be	
We're far enough to raise a light	Where are your matches?	Something big and wet
I brought a lamp	It's awfully dark here	is on my foot
There	The light doesn't make me	It's just a toad
Now we can see the trail well enough	feel better	
	The forest doesn't look better by lamplight	
Can you hear the forest?		

Tasi	Lua	Tolu
	You say that like it was a person	It's beautiful
It is a person		I can hear the forest talking
Follow me	I have to be home by a certain time	
Quiet		I can see the moon
Let me blow out the light	It doesn't look like	
Wait		The moon is so big
		So big it looks like it's falling
	It is falling	
The moon is falling		The moon is falling
Hold hands!	The moon is falling	The moon is falling
Hold hands		
Circle. Circle. Circle	The air is turning round with bats	The moon is here
Circle. Circle. Circle	There are bats everywhere	The moon! The moon!
Circle. Circle. Circle	Circle. Circle. Circle	The moon!

The Seventh Wave

Come not on the first unfolding wave
It will rush you to an early grave
And crush your heart on the reef

Wait out the third wave patiently
It wants to take you down and back to sea
In pieces, as a dish
For wild fish

The fifth wave makes us invisible
So for each other let us be careful

Listen to the shells sigh on the prow
Descend the glass of the seventh wave
Ride your keel fly fast
Come in to me
In to me

Turtle Island Poem Number One

A savage morning
   the blinds shut
do you really prefer sleeping with cats
   the moon in someone's coffee cup
the locked gate
   the lost keys
that he unlocked
   that I found I left them on the bookshelf
torn pieces of thread
   all our red flesh memory
blankets of flesh
   blankets of blood
bones and the sea
   carrying us west
the sun drowning
   the sea filled with rainbows
memories scattered
   dew on the sleeve

Turtle Island Poem Number Two

You lose a photograph
you lose it on a walk
you wish you hadn't
ended up in hot tub
        at three a.m.
        with the queen of glitter bands

e le fia
le fiafiaga
skip skip, e fia
from every hillside
let freedom ding

acjachemem
acjachemem
        the land breeze blows back again
        against the wind from the sea
the faint shadow of yourself cast by the sun reflected from a building
the marks you leave
on his skin

again
the moon escapes detection
Geiger counter
static cling
radio starlight
        ding
        in acjachemem
        ding

Turtle Island Poem Number Three

A dead ringer
Bumping into someone
A slip
Shoo fly, shoo

A dead ringer
Rubbing out a painting
From left to right
Turning with the sun

A dead ringer
A slip
Made of lace
A mirror
Of seawater
A light
Memory

Darkness
Of

Turtle Island Poem Number Four

I was in Washington DC
By accident, looking at Yves Klein
Blue sponges
Blue Arman
Rose sponges
Blue rain
Blue powder
Blue prints of women, why?
Why the Washington monument?
Washington DC like Pago Pago somehow but an African American city
It was a hundred degrees today
The pool in front of the Capitol empty
I was disappointed in Titian
At the National Gallery
And then not
I was not disappointed in El Greco
And then I was
Tonight I missed my connecting flight
And ended up in Arlington Texas
I met a cowboy
A horse trainer
With a handlebar moustache
I can't seem to spell moustache right
I had to talk like him for him to understand me
Yes sir I sure did
In a couple hours the sky will shine Yves Klein blue
On this big white bed

Turtle Island Poem Number Five

Fa'afafine me
Fa'afafine you
Fa'afafine kiss
       and kiss back

Fa'afafine shade
Fa'afafine shine
Fa'afafine never
       ever never whine

Fa'afafine mat
Fa'afafine oh something like that
       so when I was leaving Texas
       I was talking to this other guy
       and I said how do you like living in Texas
       and he said it's alright
       and I said but what about all the red(neck)s
       and he said well they still practice the 3 Ks
       and I thought to myself, the three Ks what's that?
Kindness, uh, what else
       Oh, I said, you mean the Ku Klux Klan?
       I thought the FBI got rid of them or something
Don't you believe it, he said
       they're still here
Do you think the Bush family are KKK, I asked?
Probably, he said

Fa'afafine fly
Fa'afafine bye

Turtle Island Poem Number Six

nothing is natural
nothing is normal
except we make it so

call me a betch
you betcha

the same goes for unnatural
the same goes for the weird

from a car the landscape is moving
from the landscape a car is blah
it's all tumbling in nothing
to nothing
making light

can i tickle you from here
that is this industry

samoa
hawaiki
pulotu
so far
far away

somewhere between
you or me

Turtle Island Poem Number Seven

from the top of alta laguna the hillsides curve and fold in sage and mustard, chalk filling
our shoes
in newport bay the sails cup and luff against the halyards, sea salt coating my glasses
on the freeway seven lanes south seven lanes north in saddleback valley light dims beneath
    huge gray military copters overhead one each side of the freeway the idols of war

Turtle Island Poem Number Eight

what is the west?
asia is west of samoa
america is east of samoa
europe is the far east
the west is a mirroring glass
the east is a glassy mirror

my tuaʻā went east from samoa to america
to hollywood that westernmost american factory
your tuaʻā went west from samoa to australia
to new south wales, new? wales?

when i was young my tamā held me by the balls and blessed my hide for fucking another boy
he built nine towns in nevada to be blown up in atomic bomb tests, tethered horses at
various distances
he and his squad defused yet unexploded bombs in saigon buildings delicately
he knew mountain villages of laos like islands of home, surveyed rivers of danang
now i give care for him in acjachemem laguna beach with my tuafafine
his memories leaving him like soap bubbles
singing old pese hymns at nightfall

we were our own space ship to ourselves
in nippon deutschland españa lafrance
in ohlone acjachemem hawaiinei and samoaʻisasaʻe
my tamā a distant sun
in alaska pueblo thai kampuchea vietnam
my tinā the lunar spaceship sina
denying our culture like a good christian
but she returned to samoa the path to pulotu
in the end
in this dark i see the light of her path

Turtle Island Poem Number Nine

it's the fourth of july
champagne headache
municipal fireworks in the distance
san clemente
dana point
laguna beach
newport beach
dimly past newport, long beach
and far out to sea catalina island
the inland cities reflected on the clouds

somewhere the dark ships wait
to take us back
the ones that brought us here
falling out of the sky
plank by plank
body by body
cathedrals falling apart
heart by heart
soifua

Turtle Island Poem Number Ten

swing

       eye
swing

       sky
swing

       bye
swing

       high
swing

       lie
swing

       nigh
swing

       sigh
swing

       cry
swing

       guy
swing

       pie
swing

Turtle Island Poem Number Eleven

dearest
when blowing conch remember anything
hide your teeth except where chewing notes
a drop of olive oil doesn't hurt or
skin music is sacred but a clean one is just as
meeting of minds, his conch and somewhere yours
so it helps to be an artist and intellectual it
your tongue is the wave all surfers
your lips are as interesting as la belle hum
your throat is a very
and breathe

Turtle Island Poem Number Twelve

from an old fa'agogo chant

The arrow of Sina struck—a first seaward
The arrow of Sina struck—a first to land
Again Sina's arrow struck—first at sea
There was no other woman
        quite like her
        skin anointed by kinswomen
        singing at her back
        as dawn rose over eastern Saua
Sina saw
        the white fairy tern
        who pivots on the tide
        and called out

"My husband, my white fairy tern
        take my love on the tips of your wings"

And the village called,
        "Boys, come gather, seek far for Sina's husband"
And they called to Sina,
        "Moonlight, come here
        now sit in here
        and we will be the messengers
        to your white fairy
        even though you missed his flight
        Sina, darling, don't go on so"

And they went after him

Turtle Island Poem Number Thirteen

yesterday we took a walk
down the street
you found some boxes
and down the sea staire
across the tracks
north along the strand
to the pier
halfway you went inside
outside i watched two young surfers
paddle to the edge of the reef
where fishing boats wander
and a lone fisher walked out of the ocean
trying to sell a giant bass on his speargun

on the way back
the coast surfliner whistled going north
every once in a while it runs someone over
you found a piece of sea smooth glass
rare now glass is not allowed on the beach
so home again
but never again the same bed
walking up the hill we
went inland, as an old poet once sang
where tagaloa sleeps

Turtle Island Poem Number Fourteen

once i left turtle island and i
rejoined la and doubleU and see
to savai'i on a hunting trip
on the fairy from upolu
la picked up a day trick
blew him during lunch
on the beach under a tree
in front of some australian girls
and an old couple from germany
who politely ignored us
while doubleU and see and i
made afternoon conversation
when we got to la's beach house
that night la wanted us
to share her trick like a joint
there was nearly an argument
but doubleU and i took the truck instead
and a case of beer, 'ua ka se fia?
ka se fia? leai. leai. leai. sole!
met some fishermen
i set my sights on the one who
looked like tall samoan jesus
although the little lead fisherman chose me instead
at the beach house we played the game
of love, girls on our side
boys their side
la's day trick already
disappeared, at some point that night
la's aunt and girl cousin dropped by
and la pushed me and my two fishermen
into one of the darkened bedrooms
we made love silently the three of us
while la talked loudly in the kitchen
with his aunt and cousin
when the kinswomen left
la and doubleU came in to comment
on my lovemaking performance like film critics
i smiled but they took jesus away
that's when i realized the little fisherman
who stayed sending them off
was the most

beautiful
boy
  i'd ever met, some times
it takes a while
to realize this about
            some
                one

Turtle Island Poem Number Fifteen

i met john cage
when i was nineteen in turtle island
he spoke sitting by a small table with a large bottle of fine red wine and a wine glass he
kept filling and sipping
he talked as long as it took to finish the bottle
i remember he laughed a lot, while i sat at his feet
that week there was a performance of winter music, twelve? pianos on the balconies and
floor
a big white shag rug in the middle and we lay there listening to winter music for ten?
pianos
joan la barbara
                    sang

in spite of which
i ran from turtle island
leaving a black siapo dot behind
never leaving turtle island
i ran into a stranger piano
prepared with flotsam and jetsam
hermitage, a shell containing
a shadow, no, a tidal pool reflection
of samoa

In Suva

In Suva
>the buses rumble, rumble, rumble
>>cough, cough, cough

In Suva
>the grass grows tall
>>houses grow between houses

In Suva
>Lani paints the ocean in her hair
>>sea green, sea blue

In Suva
>Rusi paints a fist
>>and I go, Ouch

In Suva
>Filipe and the guys carve
>>the thirty-two teeth of Tangaloa

In Suva
>Epeli
>>is here, there
>>>and everywhere

In Suva
>Tere looks twenty
>>on her fortieth birthday
>>>is she a witch?

In Suva
>Tevi raises us high, high, high
>>with kava, kava, kava

In Suva
>Jazz
>>handles
>>>her
>>>>shit

In Suva
>Sinu dances in the air
>and Glenville, Pelu, Etu, Nisi, Kata, Ateca, Sachan, and always Tulevu
>like birds, birds, birds

In Suva
>Lani teaches me to weave a Suva lei

>make a basket with your hands
>>gather left

                                        gather right
                                                gather forward

and wear it here
            (around the collar)
wear it here
            (at the heart)
wear it here
            (on the ear)
alofa atu
        loloma

Laguna Beach Poem Number One

Miss Thing's my imaginary lover
She drives me everywhere
Up hill and down
To the edge of despair

Miss Thing's my imaginary friend
She cooks all with love
I shiver and shake
When her wings shine above

Miss Thing's my imaginary husband
As young as can be
If eternity were an hour
And now she has me

Miss Thing's my imaginary heart
And I her favorite freak
Tho to hear us talk would bore you
It's not for you we speak

Miss Thing's my imaginary boyfriend
My bridge from toe to crown
I would have, if I left her
A change of mind falling down

Laguna Beach Poem Number Two

Yesterday it was the battle of the Windward
                                                   (Flutters a hand before her face)
Versus the Leeward
                              (Flutters a hand behind her)

Today it's the battle of the Iron Fist
                                              (Makes a fist in the air)
Versus the Feather of Language
                                          (Opens fist to blow a kiss)

Laguna Beach Poem Number Three

Do you know the warrior goddess Nafanua?
They say she killed many men

Maybe the men killed themselves for her
All those beautiful heads buried in her malae

    (The taupou runs her hands in a circle along the inside of the 'ava bowl)

They were lovers not fighters

    (The taupou tosses the used fau away over her shoulder)

Can I get an Amene?

Laguna Beach Poem Number Four

I have a friend, Jesus
He's such a liar

That man lies and lies and lies and lies
And his name is Jesus
Which is so wrong

If I say
     Fucking Orange County
He says
       I am

Laguna Beach Poem Number Five

I hope you don't mind,
                      I'm a faleaitu
Everything I say is a joke

Like
    marry me

Marry me
Be my husband or my wife
                      tonight

And always
If we can
If they don't stop us
If they will marry us
Then marry me

Laguna Beach Poem Number Six

I'm a winner, I mean, sinner
I'm blessed, I mean, damned
I'm going to fresh Hell, I mean, Paradise
They love me there

But why must I wait for night?

A Drag Queen Named Pipi (at the Bone Bar)

Shoulder to shoulder
My sisters and I
Holding our heads high
Filing through the bone bar
Pass the hollow beds
Don't fall in!
We're just here to steal wreaths
To share with the living
Don't mind us
Don't fall in, we whisper loudly
We'd only follow you
Single file dance with us into the bone bar
Meeting your sons after shut down elsewhere
When real girls go home
When police close those others
And join us and the moon in her white garden
Singing lip to lip at the bone bar
Haunted by dogs, your sons
Our babies

Pray

Pray for both Tuna and Fata the orators say
Talo lua Tuna ma Fata
Play with both Tuna and Fata my boyfriend said
Taalo lua Tuna ma Fata

Young man works the family plantation
Captains rugby for the village team
Wears his best game shirt come Saturday
My pe'u, my manamea

Relighting the ula he got at black market
If I should take a notion to jump into the ocean
Ain't nobody's business if I do
Stretched out in my panties

On the teak table ufi and talo among the candles
Fresh baked from the farm in coconut milk wrapped with leaves
He brought on the bus with his friend to me
And a bottle of vodka our 'ava

Ufi and talo in coconut milk
Ain't nobody's business
                              but my own

Fa'a Fafine Poem Number One

Am I a Fafine
Who is caught in a Fa'a life?

Or am I a Fa'a
Who is caught in a Fafine life?

Fa'a Fafine Poem Number Two

I first knew the art of painting by the smell of 'o'a
        juice of the blood tree bright orange
        in white lacquered tin bowls nailed to the bark
        filled with color and the scent of 'o'a
        down the path through the rainforest
        to greatgrandma and grandma's fale
Fa'asapa and Sisipeni

        one doesn't forget the smell of 'o'a
        or coconut oil on old ladies' arms
        walking on their legs to massage them
Fa'asapa as thin and dark and hard as a fau hibiscus tree
        delicate in her gentleness, a hundred years old
She took her 'upeti board and brushed on soga
        to keep the bark cloth from sticking
Now working in oil paints the smell of the oils
        is pungent to remind me of fresh 'o'a and soga

Sisipeni, my grandma, stout and white haired
        ironed with a flat iron on a small coal brazier
        sewed embroidery on pillow slips. 'Aluga patterns
        Bibles and hibiscus flowers
        proverbs in Samoan in gothic letters

            there is a day that never ends
            a small child and
            two old women

Fa'a Fafine Poem Number Three

In the old stories, there is always a couple
Whose children all have the same name
If it was Fatu, they were all called Fatu
If it was 'Ele'ele, they were all 'Ele'ele

Until something memorable occurred
Then each received their very own name

When I became a poet I renamed myself Taulaitu, demon anchor
When my mother named me Taulapapa,
And we cannot name ourselves

Generations generations ago a young woman, married to an important walking ulcer, ran away with his nephew
And their ship could find no shelter except a cliff, papa, to which they anchored, taula
They had a child there Taulapapa, from whom both my parents descended
Our lines come from the black sky and from the deep black sea

Fa'a Fafine Poem Number Four

At a church in Edinburgh
        thousands of missionary children gathered in a hall
        decked with idols suspended from the roof
Stone, wooden, and woven shadows of the worshipped
        cast in the fires of Europe
While their souls fled where?
Into what dark pit hole of Hell?

Here where their shadows weave
Here I weave
        a taulaitu

They say Hell is a bad naughty hole
A church going blood once informed me that I'm a hole
Something we had in common
Recently a painter in L.A. she said to me, Oh the hole is a source of pleasure!
Besides, we were all born in sacred holes
I'm a hole, you're a hole
Life is sweet like
Sugar cane

Fa'a Fafine Poem Number Five

When we moved from the United States Territory of American Samoa
        to the United States of America, I, a small fa'afafine child
        should act like an American boy because we were not in Samoa any more
But I met an older Cuban boy who showed me his boner holder and fell in love making
        until our fathers, both drill sergeants, found out and I was the one blamed
        dancing naked about the bathtub in a shower of leather whacks
        kicked out wandering that night, spit on by the other boys on bikes
        falling asleep outside the front door until my mother and sisters came down
the stairs

When no one was looking standing on my toes I kissed the painting of Jesus beautiful
English face
I kissed him on his red red lips again and again, with his rosy white movie star skin and
black Irish hair
His kisses forgave me filled me with American peace and love
Among the fa'afafine immigrants in the United States
        as children girls in Samoa
        as adults Gay American men, giving you
        this, the surface

Fa'a Fafine Poem Number Six

"were it not for English war ships
                              and occasional displays of naval force
few missionaries or traders in these archipelagoes
                              would lay
them down at night
                    with untroubled minds

The gunboats of Great Britain are constantly engaged
                                        in police service
throughout these seas
                      prowling from place to place
appearing unexpectedly here and there
                                    and often being called upon
to make a demonstration of force
                          in order to keep the natives
                                              on their good behavior
. . . the leaven of barbarism still remains
                              everywhere
and if British guns were withdrawn both
                                  mission stations
and trade factories would not
                    long survive"

—*Fiji Times*, 19th century

The gunboats still
                police

Fa'a Fafine Poem Number Seven

One evening
> at the end of a jaunt around
> the island of Savai'i with some fa'afafine friends
> recovering from the hunt, having dinner at a beach rental
> our landlady who was a lo'omatua
> an old woman
> waggling her long forefinger under my nose
> said to me

"You're loose
> like an old woman"

Fa'a Fafine Poem Number Eight

At church
        cousin She
        born J
        dresses in white
        long white dress
        billowy white blouse
        large shady white hat with white lace
        white heels and a white woven fan
Despite the failed attempt among fundamentalists in Samoa
        influenced by American televangelism
        to force fa'afafine to dress as men in church
Fa'afafine do always dress as ladies in the choir
        as businesswomen at work
        as Miss at the chalkboard
        as Mom at the shop
        as Aunty at home

Fa'a Fafine Poem Number Nine

Once I moved to a village far from my relations
       and met my first male lover in Samoa, F
        while renting an apartment from a friend who had a store next door
The first night I saw my lover he walked in the shop in just
       an 'ie lavalava cinched tight at his narrow waist
       his background was like a bookshelf, you could bounce a car off it
       body shiny with coconut oil scenting broad rugby shoulders
       and his black black curly hair

For a week after work in just his mechanic overalls unbuttoned to his taut belly
       he came every day to the store to talk in Samoan to my friend
       his bright shining eyes ignoring me
       a week I could hardly breathe

Then Sunday afternoon I heard him drumming his knuckles on the wall to my door
       I opened to see
He stood there as the village slept

"Do you have a secret place?"
       he asked
So he spoke English
       "No," I pouted

       "I said do you have a cigarette?"
He said like I misheard him
I rolled my eyes, "No"
He stared
I stared
And turned in a stroll to my bed
        left the door wide open . . .

Growing up in an assimilated Samoan American Republican born again fundamentalist
family
       I was dead silent at the usual village talks
Until my landlady had a first year birthday party for her son
       and the women of the village showed up in force

When I approached the buffet
        an old woman did a little dance
           waving a banana slowly in my face

       the rest laughed and I breathed
The homophobia of my old family
        fading
        into blue

Fa'a Fafine Poem Number Ten

In the English Bible it is written
"Thou shalt not lie down with mankind
        as with womankind
        it is an abomination"

In the Samoan Tusi Pa'ia it is written
"Aua lua te momoe ma se tane
        e pei ona momoe ma se fafine
        o le mea e inosia lava lea"

Thus it is written that a tane cannot sleep with a tane
        but it is not written that a tane cannot sleep with a fa'afafine

Fa'a Fafine Poem Number Eleven

I went to the beach in a small hired bus
      with a group of fa'afafine friends on Christmas day
      the drunken driver careening
      down the narrow sandy road
      crashing through branches of the rainforest
      as everyone sang Samoan pese hymns
      exchanging puns of the body for verses

I was talking with a Tongan scholar OM who told me about a conversation
      he had with the Samoan writer AW
That before Christianity came to the South Pacific islands
      curses were directed at the other's family
But with Christianity, curses are directed to the other's
                             body

Fa'a Fafine Poem Number Twelve

I was at home in Apia, Samoa, about to visit a village in Manu'a
A friend K suggested I stay with his mother Fa'amanu, which I did

Fa'amanu in the afternoon liked to sit on a nicely woven mat with her small granddaughter
      in her family meeting house, a lovely round little building
      without walls, just round white pillars

Fa'amanu was the local expert in the weaving of 'ie toga or Samoan fine mats
Her practice was walking around the village advising, encouraging
      young women at their weaving

Her inner forearms were scarred with diagonal lines
      from the sharp pandanus leaves she gathered

Every sunset during my stay, Fa'amanu and her little granddaughter and I
      took a stroll round the village talking with neighbors

Some of the women neighbors had a very friendly relationship with her
      some pointedly ignored her with a harumph, turning to their gardening siva
nofo, and
      some of the men seemed to have intimate friendships with her, the language of
their bodies
          suddenly youthful again in a walking dance of greeting, she in front
          his brown hands gently on her brown shoulders

When I returned to Apia, a friend M asked who I stayed with, and I said
      "Our friend K's mother, Fa'amanu"
To which M remarked, "His mother?
      His parents died when he was young, he was brought up by a fa'afafine"

Fa'amanu wanted me to learn how to weave fine mats, a woman's art
      and I said I'd come back
She said, "Don't wait, our time is short"

And a year or two later she took the last journey
      I didn't return in time to revisit my elder
            or learn the perfection of her art but
Her walk is my walk
      too

Fa'a Fafine Poem Number Thirteen

Treasure Island's Robert Louis Stevenson
        spent his last years building a home, Vailima
        in the hills above Apia

In his other travel book, there's a passage
        where a young island guy follows him to the forest, and
        in its dark gives him a carved box inside of which
        is a smaller carved copy of the box

At tea in Apia once, M told me that at Vailima, where
        she grew up
        Stevenson kept a house in back
        where he would meet
                the island boys he came for
                        at last, home

From the
        sea

Fa'a Fafine Poem Number Fourteen

A New Zealand professor warned us in her book that if
        fa'afafine don't take on Western gender and sexuality terminology
        we will be more susceptible to AIDS

This reminds one of nineteenth-century European/American missionaries
        who told Pacific Islanders that the cure for Western diseases was
        Western religion

Fa'a Fafine Poem Number Fifteen

Midnight mass, Christmas Eve, the cathedral in Tafuna, Tutuila island
        American Samoa

Invited by my Aunt L and her daughters
        my cousins, white lace covering their hair

Outside the church
        a group of ancient white priests from who knows where
        paraded in procession
        bent covert bodies in elaborate robes

They were preceded and followed by about forty Samoan altar boys in scant
        mini skirt lavalava wrapped around their waists with nothing else
        barefoot, shiny bodies covered in coconut oil, carrying tall candles
It was a Roman scene like the ink drawings of Aubrey Beardsley

During the service the white Archbishop of the South Pacific spoke
        in Samoan with an aesthete voice
        looking and sounding like Peter Cook imitating the Archbishop of Canterbury
        he sermoned in a tongue wrinkled and powdered

Fa'a Fafine Poem Number Sixteen

Missionary Rev P: "The greatest favorite was the Poula
        This was an obscene night dance
        and a constant source of
                enjoyment

"The only covering of the males consisted of the titi, or girdle of leaves
        often not more than seven or eight inches in width, and about the same in depth

        whilst that of the females consisted of a white or red shaggy mat around the loins
        the upper part of the body being
                uncovered

"Both sexes paid great attention to their hair
        that of the males being long and allowed to hang loosely over the shoulders

        whilst the females, who wore their hair short, stiffened it with pulu, breadfruit pitch
        or else dressed it with a pomade of a certain kind of light-colored clay, which
        was afterwards washed off with lime water, thus dyeing the hair to
        a much-coveted brown
                color

"The last dance . . . when this skilled dance concluded
        the males who had danced exchanged girdles, and
        commenced a variety of antics and buffoonery which formed
        a prelude to the closing saturnalia

        of which a description is
                inadmissible
                  here, but

        which was always received with shouts of laughter and approval"

Fa'a Fafine Poem Number Seventeen

I had a husband M in Apia who came home after work
        throwing off his clothes
        putting on just an 'ie lavalava
        so aulelei

He cooked dinner
        fish in coconut milk
After dinner we'd sit on low rattan chairs across from each
        other at the low teak table, candles on the table lighting the room
He turned on Radio 2AP, the traditional Samoan music station, to
        dance a siva nofo, sitting dance, to me

He taught me the movements of the taupou, girl chief
He made the movements of the manaia, boy chief
His hand movements would end up caressing his exposed
                        erection
Pull me in and push me away with his gestures
Push pull, push pull
Back and forth

And I'd respond in my dance
But we didn't
      touch
        each
          other
            all
              evening
Until at some undetermined point
                  we broke the tension and
        rushed to the next and darkened room to
                  our bed
                      under its fairy net

One day my neighbor told me she and her girlfriend would
        sit at the farthest reach of her orchid garden
                  in the dark
        smoke a number, sip their wine, and watch
        my beautiful young husband through our lanai screens
        dancing naked by candlelight

He told me then he always knew
                when they were watching
This was our village
        Po
          Ula

Fa'a Fafine Poem Number Eighteen

Margaret Mead when she first came to Samoa stayed as a lodger with
        my aunt Helen in Leone on my father's side
Mead and Aunty Helen didn't like each other

My aunt didn't like Mead asking her children so many questions
        and complaining about the rent

Aunty Helen's daughter, my aunt Tutasi, remembers collecting shells
        at a penny each for Mead, who threw the shellfish behind her dresser to make
a stink

Later Mead went to Ta'u in Manu'a where my mother's side is, and
        there Margaret Mead did her studies of young Samoan girls, but
        this time she questioned them on the porch of the Naval Dispensary
        as a US government official

Once when I stayed in Ta'u I took an early morning walk on the beach
There was a guy fishing. When he saw me getting near he signaled and
        a young man and woman tangled in the beach vines stood and walked
        casually in opposite directions, the young woman pulling leaves out of her hair
        yanking up her blouse

I thought of Mead
She was a kind of missionary, supported by gunboats, with
        a covert love for the Po Ula of life
        which local Samoans say she found in the vines
        and among the trees
                    at night

Fa'a Fafine Poem Number Nineteen

Leader of the anti-homosexual marriage movement in Hawaiinei is Samoan
       a politician whose sibling is queer
Whom I saw in the airport smiling back from a family reunion
       took a partner to the reunion, but not out in public
Condemned aspects of my work in private in ink as anti-Samoan
       we kissed and parted smiling waving
I walked away with flowers gave me
       some food stared at

Fa'a Fafine Poem Number Twenty

In Apia
        for my accent
        my friends named me Miss America

Until seeing me coming out of the only McDonald's in Samoa
        as none of them would eat there
        the imported prices, tourist brags
        for my poor habit, they called me Cookie Monster

Elder now, a shorter friend calls Granny Tranny to me
A name is like a sei, the power flower on one's ear
Maybe someone gives it to you but they are the ones who see it
A sei by any other name is a sei
                is a sei is
                    a sei

Fa'a Fafine Poem Number Twenty-One

The Samoan leader of the anti-gay movement in New Zealand said
    "Oh clearly there were a number of us that had Christian values
    and therefore we fell in opposition to some of the views and agendas
    that certain people in caucus had, particularly in regard to moral issues
    There's no question about that"

He was later convicted on bribery and corruption charges
                                          based on actions in office

Fa'a Fafine Poem Number Twenty-Two

"Teaching the people of Samoa Christianity through the Graceland
      Broadcasting Network"
      Sponsored by Channel 40 from Santa Ana, California
      our family in the television audience, phone volunteers, pilgrims

After its establishment on Savai'i Island in Samoa
      there was a case of two young women on the island who were
                                             lovers
The family of one of them on discovering the relationship
                                beat their daughter badly
      and she ended up hanging herself
                         The other young woman
      on learning of her lover's suicide
                       committed suicide herself by
      swallowing the poison Paraquat
                   After a mention in the newspaper
      the issue was buried with
              the young women

      but among faatane shooting pool in Apia bars
                        you hear
                           of this couple

Fa'a Fafine Poem Number Twenty-Three

Nafanua was the greatest warrior of Samoan history
             When she went to war (s)he disguised her gender by covering her chest

One day in battle her covering was torn off and her sex was discovered
When she retired from fighting she became an advocate of peaceful discourse
      and influenced the ways Samoans conduct politics in
                        the fono
      communal meeting house for the fa'amatai system of decentralized governance
      and communal land ownership
After her death she was deified
              made a goddess
As the goddess Nafanua she spoke to Samoa through talking chiefs
      on the island of Savai'i. Through these talking chiefs she predicted
      the coming of Christianity to Samoa, so the converts
                    say

Fa'a Fafine Poem Number Twenty-Four

A few years ago I was invited to go with Team Papua New Guinea, Team Fiji,
        Team Tonga, and Team Samoa to the Gay Games in Sydney
I went as a poet to the games indigenous arts festival that
        the Aboriginal Australians and Torres Straits Islanders sponsored
        while most of our fa'afafine Team Samoa were net ball players and swimmers
        in their early twenties

They arrived in Sydney with empty bags and went to the corner of Kings Cross and
        in a week there were limousines pulling up to the building and
        men in tuxedos escorting the young fa'afafine around town and
        flying them to other cities and
        half of us overstayed

At the Opening Ceremonies at Sydney Stadium, all
        the other queer teams marched
                in formation
        wearing regulation uniforms for their countries

Team Samoa was the only team at the Gay Games
                in drag

The local Aboriginal, Maori, and Pacific Islander families in force gave us spontaneous
haka
    tributes from the stands

The young fa'afafine dressed me up as the lo'omatua, pushing me ahead
        a fine mat around my chest and
        some feathers knocking against my forehead

When I walked on the field there was a Samoan cameraman waving
        I waved back
On the giant screen amid the cheering crowds
        an older fa'afafine in close-up was nodding quaintly
        Oh gawd, I thought, she's
                me

Fuck it, I said, and did a
        catwalk stroll
      in a big loop across the great field

One by one the younger fa'afafine followed in heels or on their toes
                                                    beautifully

Tall dark drag queens in
                        silver two-piece bathing suits
                with high tuiga headdresses of
                                        orange feathers
                like Las Vegas showgirls
                smiling and waving
                at Australia

The Bat

Once upon a time in old Pulotu
                        there were two fa'afafine named Muli and Pipi

Pipi was pretty
            but Muli knew how to talk

Every night they walked the beaches
                        looking for sailors

In those days everyone in Pulotu was a sailor

When they found one, they had their way with him
because
            they never did each other
                        one of those things

Afterwards
            as the islands used to be dens of cannibalism
one of them hit the nodding sailor with a rock
                        and they devoured him

They did this until there were no more young men left
                        on their little island

In fact by this time
Pipi had really learned everything she would from Muli
and Muli was starting to desire Pipi
so they did each other

                    but afterwards Pipi killed Muli
                            and devoured her
as people who come to one for advice will

This act made the gods very angry at Pipi
                    so for punishment they turned her into a bat

For years Pipi flew up and down the beach at night
                    on little leather wings

There were no young men
until finally the Americans landed

Pipi's first white man
                              but she knew a sailor when she saw one

Pipi sunk her teeth into the sailor's fat neck
                                             and the sailor fainted
Then Pipi drank until she got plump and passed out

When she woke up she was in a basket aboard a ship
and ended up at University of Minnesota Medical School
where she was given a nice warm cage
                              by a local foundation

One day
I'm not sure how but I'll let you know
                              she escaped
It was the especially cold winter of '94
                              eighteen-ninety-four

Pipi flew above the buildings
and south over the pale northern Mississippi River landscape
It was snowing
and everything was white

Suddenly far below she saw something in black leather

Flying down she discovered a boot
that some young man had left there the previous summer
along with his glasses and a pair of shorts he lost
along the river bank
walking to the corner store late one night
fetching a bottle of milk for the wife and five kids

By now Pipi's wings had frozen and she was stuck

She was in love with the black leather boot
                              although it didn't speak
and she couldn't eat it

She didn't think she could eat it
                    and love it

The snow kept falling
                    until it covered them both like a blanket

The end

Postscript

I began publishing poems in the mid-90s while living in Minneapolis, Minnesota, where "J, She, and the Eel," and "The Bat," the poems that begin and end this book, were written—memories of Samoa interrogated by Midwest winter. Some of these poems were written recently in the Laguna Hills in California; the rest while living in Apia in Samoa-i-Sisifo; in Leone village in Samoa-i-Sasaʻe; in San Francisco, California; in Christchurch, Aotearoa; and in Suva, Viti.

Malo lava to Craig Santos Perez, without whose support this book could not have happened, and deep thanks to Craig and to Brandy Nālani McDougall for their kind, insightful, and patient editing of this volume, and for their support of Pacific Islander poets through the University of Hawaiʻi's Native Voices performance series and as the publishers of Ala Press.

Faʻafetai tele lava to friends whose mana influenced this work: Sia Figiel, Albert Wendt, Shigeyuki Kihara, Brian Fuata, Allan Alo, Karin Williams, Richard Kereopa, Noelani Arista, Christine Kunewa Walker, Teresia Teaiwa, Keith Camacho, Victor Rodger, Ibrahim Farajajé, Russ Butler, Joël Barraquiel Tan, Kehaulani Kauanui, Lisa Kahaleole Hall, Frank Wilderson, Ema Tavola, Dionne Fonoti, Mohit Prasad, Elizabeth DeLoughrey, Marco Larsen , Ken Moala, and Stephen Dunn; and both the late Merata Mita and the late Epeli Hauʻofa, who inspire us in the Pacific.

Faʻafetai to my aiga for your alofa and in loving memory of our parents Lupelele Iosefa McMullin and Samuelu Sailele McMullin. Tulou, tulou lava.

Faʻafetai tele lava to our faʻafafine community, Utopia San Francisco, and the Samoa Faʻafafine Organisation.

Thank you to the institutions that supported the work during these writings, including: American Samoa Council on Culture, Arts, and Humanities, National University of Samoa, American Samoa Community College, University of the South Pacific Oceania Centre for the Arts, University of Hawaiʻi Center for Pacific Islands Studies and English Department, Pacific Islanders in Communications, Claremont Graduate University Art Department, University of California Los Angeles Pacific Islands Students Association, University of Canterbury MacMillan Brown Centre for Pacific Studies, University of Michigan Asian/Pacific Islander American Studies program, Victoria University of Wellington Pacific Islands Studies, Waiariki Institute of Technology Art Department, California State University Long Beach Pacific Islanders Student Association, University of California Irvine Humanities and Arts Department, Bates College Multicultural Center, Columbia University, New York University, Keomailani Hanapi Foundation, Pacific Festival of the Arts, Pacific Arts Association, de Young Museum African and Oceania Collections, Okai Reef Gallery, Fresh Gallery Otara, University of California Davis Gorman Museum Ethnic/Native American Studies, Pacific Island Ethnic Museum, Sundance Institute's Native American and Indigenous Program, Writers Guild of America Indigenous Screenwriters Lab, California Arts Council, The Writer's Loft, The Playwrights' Center, The Jerome Foundation, The McKnight Foundation, Mid Atlantic Arts Foundation, Samoan

Community Development Center, Djerassi Artist Colony, the LGBT Centers of San Francisco and Los Angeles, and Gay Games Sydney Aboriginal Arts Festival.

Previous versions of some of these poems were published in the following book anthologies (including a chapbook of my early poems), for which I thank the editors involved: *A Drag Queen Named Pipi*, Tinfish Press of Honolulu, series ed. Susan Schultz; *Nafanua: Poetry and Plays from the 11th Quadrennial Festival of Pacific Arts*, Ala Press, ed. Craig Santos Perez and Brandy Nālani McDougall; *Whetu Moana: Polynesian Poetry in English* and *Mauri Ola: Contemporary Polynesian Poems in English*, ed. Albert Wendt, Reina Whaitiri, and Robert Sullivan; *Without Reservation: Indigenous Erotica*, ed. Kateri Akiwenzie-Damm; *Sovereign Erotics: A Collection of Two-Spirit Literature* (First Peoples: New Directions in Indigenous Studies), ed. Daniel Heath Justice, Deborah Miranda, Lisa Tatonetti, and Qwo-Li Driskill; *Queer Indigenous Studies: Critical Interventions in Theory, Politics and Literature* (First Peoples: New Directions in Indigenous Studies), ed. Chris Finley, Brian Joseph Gilley, Qwo-Li Driskill, and Scott Lauria Morgensen; *Take Out: Queer Writing from Asian Pacific America* (Asian American Writers Workshop), ed. Quang Bao. And thanks to the editors of UCLA's *Amerasia Journal*, ed. Keith Camacho and Arnold Pan; *Achiote Seeds*, ed. Craig Santos Perez; *Bamboo Ridge*, ed. Darrel Lum and Eric Chock; *Trout*, ed. Tony Murrow; *Folauga*, ed. Don Long; *Evergreen Chronicles*, ed. Juliana Hu Pegues; and *Lavender Godzilla*, ed. Joël Barraquiel Tan.

Finally, thank you to the University of Arizona Press and editors Kristen Buckles and Susan Campbell.

About the Author

Dan Taulapapa McMullin is a poet and painter from the Samoa Islands. His work breaks new ground in contemporary Polynesian verse, rejecting the Hollywood notion that indigenous communal societies are abject, colonized, and struggling to remain in a fictional past. His paintings and poems cross lines of gender, nationality, and media.